My Original Enthusiasm

Lori Lubeski

My Original Enthusiasm

I.

I can't sleep
on account of
being left behind

Who testifies
that Little Rock, Roxbury
deserve armed guards of duty
howling intimacy
incites surgery
backbone wet
with anesthesia
my mother
has cast
an ancient spell
during the relatively ugly
birth of my
pronoun
deluded other
who infiltrated

intended womb
robbed me of
required neurons
for flight or flounder
fear or fixation
tree from father
founder and ill equipped
to grasp important
facts

I am carried out
of the classroom
on a stretcher
lips frozen
from the burden
of trying to form
a sentence

can't cry

can't identify

neither Mr. Brown

nor the bored

who has gathered up

firewood

set ablaze

the dark corridor

of transfixed nation

(nurse's station)

burning without

agitation

or

thought

II.

I can't sleep on account of
fractions

The room is spilling
and deep in
purgation
an older boy
holds a lighter
under thermometer
with clay hands
the would-be mood is sculpted

and I am driven home
with an artificially created
fever

I can't sleep

because the world is uneven

won't be divided

by insignificant pie chart

wreaking havoc

on my attention

surplus

underground railroad

signals extricable flight

of history

as I am carried away

my courage is left

resided

deep within

the vacant

bloodstream

where wolves

have once howled

in anticipation

out classroom window
bulldozers destroy
burial ground
of my mother's
childhood
backyard ablaze
with machinery
men in hard hats
pour concrete foundations
into ditch
full of arrowheads

I can't sleep
on account of
The Trail of Tears

III.

That I was suddenly
falling
left me
tumbling from
laundry basket
I returned to
my cherished body
deprived of contemplation

doctors have ambushed
the continent of my grief

told not to cry

during failure to thrive

there is a rumor
that I will plummet
from a textbook

I open my eyes
to the blindness
of my openness

when I was a child
there was a rumor
that I could not do

multiplication

IV.

After intentionally
missing the bus
walking joyfully
the miles to school

you arrive
2 hours late
candy spilling
from your pockets

distracting those
who *are actually*
trying to pay attention

nor is your internal disorder
obedient

during social studies

you crave your favorite

civilization—

the one with

indulgent boy pharaohs—

still too immature

to regard the world

as a serious matter

who played games

and loved dogs

long before

Christ

when it comes time

to replicate *beyond reproach*

a disastrous consequence

unfolds

lacking the ability

to regulate emotions

time is the terror spent

outside of your own

captivated self

faulty bloodline

destiny did not frighten

out of reappearance

swept up chivalry

of the misbehaved

we are supposed to be

learning about tundra

and savannahs

but my disassociation

prevents engagement,

inquiry, mastery—

and I am suspected aloof

in the hall of endurance

where my success is measured

by the rate of

completed tasks

instead I hear
the lone voice
of my dog:
'I was left
by the side
of the road
in a box
with my sisters
I was picked up
and de-briefed
as the setting sun
bellowed in my eyes
It was only in a trance
that I arrived
at your house,
obliterated and
unsoothed'

who would understand

the pleasure of

a dropped pacifier

on the ground

walking home from school

there is tenderness

of infancy

I was found in the morning

with a dog in my arms

twilight alive inside of me

like the hopes of Magellan

rather than

the teacher's question

instead I hear only

the sound of

long wooden oars

hitting the water

when the heart dwells

in evidence

there can only be lilacs,

soup, or the fading glimmer of jesus

rising into the waves

I can't sleep

on account of

The Spanish Inquisition

V.

The lullaby
lifts up the sleeping child
it is only in pretending
that we are carried to bed
limp chin digging into
father's shoulder blade
gentle bumping of your jaw
against his back
as he moves up each step
carefully not to wake you
yet your eyes are open

these burning episodes
appear only infrequently,
intentionally,
tenderly
as you have entered
such breaking
light
cries

VI.

Under the apple tree
we tip over inside
a refrigerator box
tumbling atop each other
in particular gleeful
abandon

my potential obeys me
when we were found falling
only into arms

that would catch us

it is there you hurry me
into morning

mistakes circled
with a red pen

mercy unfolds
like a napkin

in my lap

VII.

Building blasts time into
quadrants on a grid
I had to transpose
black and white squares
into imaginary colors
that were beyond my control
when I write my name
I am accused of forgery
were you not impeccable,
brazen,
stone's throw from my heart
calling out my name
during bold
supplemental
panic attack

when I tried to read the words

the words slipped from my vision

I surrendered

until my internal

blindness

overcomes

VIII.

(I was found in a box
on the side of the road—
kicked in and whimpering)

from your treasured disposition
I learn
tenderness of thought,
rigor of delusion

you reached in
and lifted me out

I can't sleep on account of
roman emperors

IX.

Time hangs
on an argumentative road
softened by grammar
and drinking fountain
water
classroom walls incite
mercenary strategies
to be lost or waylaid by rules
made for a different era
where decimal points
were two places to the left
and we hadn't yet learned
cursive

I can't sleep on account of
being found out

when the day consists of

zeros and incomplete worksheets

re-trace steps

back into daydreams

where the world is soft

with birdcalls and rooftops

No name

No credit

no unguarded disbelief in test questions

instead I hear only

the sound of my own

unindulged heart

throbbing

I shook hands with the principal

and the principal

let me down

I can't sleep on account of

multiple choice

PART TWO: MYTHOLOGY

I.

Be quiet and quit while you are left behind

glaringly sentimental orders

where land reaches shore and

I never understood who *really*

discovered America

swept away without words

in the tunneling melancholy

of random exploration

instead I can only imagine

the expression on the face

of the private pirate

awaiting extradition

the world rotates
on internal divinity

without regret
I have sung this song
at the risk of offending
the unenlightened
(teachers)

every word a horror story
of unimpressive dictation

In my throat
rising words
demand attention
yet I am only able to hear
the collapsing sound
of angel wings

during math class
hang your head low
so as not to be called on

when looking down
paved reflection breaks
and your desk comes
hurling at you
with utmost intensity

instead of bracing yourself
and riding it out
you imagine paramedics
tending to the wounded chief
whose throat has been
slashed
by a glorified
pilgrim

While I am being accused

of not listening

it is merely because

I can only hear

the impaled voices

of those being

forcefully marched

away from

where they

love

II.

No doubt reason shines
when a world is committed
to productivity

but I was born into a family
of images
where thunder substantiated an evening

and long lost light shining through
the kitchen window
brings the utmost joy

I am obliterated by the diligence
of the dominant culture
follow in disqualified footsteps
of gun runners and felons
staging the arena
for a free fall

when I grow up
I want to be
a Native American,
however wounded
and unholy

I want to sing
of godless hours
interrupted only

by the feeling of fingers

weaving through

strands of reed

but those daydreams become slashed

by frenzied recess duty

tumbling down

hillside alone

all of the forgetting is lost

as it leaves the mouth

in the words of the substitute teacher

who reads us the "Just So Stories"

of Rudyard Kipling

ignoring every moral

I can't sleep on account of

The Westward Expansion

III.

I can't sleep on account of
The Revolutionary War

uniformed armed guard

waits by the entrance

as we pass through

metal detector

on our way

to supposed

enlightenment

steel plate in my skull

from the glamourous aftermath

of concentration

sets off alarm

step out of line
and you will lose your place
in the jump rope competition
heart in throat anticipation of entering
perfect rhythm of swing

"My mother and your mother
were hanging out clothes
My mother punched your mother
right in the nose
what color blood came out?"

such delusional chant exists
during playground vengeance

and the journey to paradise

is more cluttered than my notebook

"Red rover, red rover, send Michael over"

silent misgivings

of unknown rituals

who does not know the difference

between geology and integrity

when I grow up

I want to be emptied

of all

I have

never

learned

gym class strengthens my ability
to sense unknown dark errors
from authority

you almost went down
but archery saved you

PART THREE: STATISTICS

I.

1 out of every
thunderous roaring
apoplectic truant officer
apologizes for inability
to perform
required duties (miracles)

when they called my mother
I pretended to be her
on the telephone
agreeing passively
to all that was uttered

when one is undermined at school
makes up lies later
to compensate

unconsciously seeks vengeance
against any
vague
explanation

I want to be let out at my bus stop

but I can't remember where it is

walk the long mile home

I can't sleep on account of

my shoes don't fit

suggestions from guidance counselors

are met with paranoia and disgust

we pity the maladjusted

in their stupor of dreams

2 out of every 4 prescription

drugs

are taken

by children

in the mouth of the dream

grasping in the dark air

unable to find

my mother's breast

I can't sleep on account of
milk money

III.

My heart plays baseball

after school but

fictitious opponent

throws me out

while I am trying to steal second

I almost went down

but Ritalin saved me

luminous contradictions

beam in the sky

set channel on

president's (principal's) speech

generates applause

while the inarticulate

burn down buildings

in frustration

looting of

store-bought homework

conspiracy up in arms

5 out of every 6 bullies

die prematurely

of heart attacks

land line lost

in commotion

stark qualities of

the aggressor

pool at my feet

while the blur of summer

distracts

every available

mind

I had to pull my brother
from the dumpster

where bullies
had thrown him

playground of
onlookers
knee deep
in seagulls

I can't sleep on account of
snow days

IV.

I can't be bribed
into testifying

while other possessed lives
scatter

the rising tide
swoons in paraphrases

because I never
learned cursive
I will be forever
unable
to rightfully
claim
my own

paranoia

your compass rules
my migraines

I have no business forging ahead
to where otherwise
lunatics
have escaped from

I can't sleep
on account of
my 63 absences

V.

When they say 'pilot'
they really mean 'plane crash'

the disgrace comes
shortly after
the apparent careless error
on the wrong side of the tracks
older kids waving me on

but I have blanked out
on the punctuation rules

and instead I am only able

to hear

the tenderness of

kisses

ricocheting

off the lucky kid's

cheek

onto

mine

when it comes time
to exchange papers
my wings are like flags
out the classroom window
I'm beckoning for your
fragrant skin cream
to deliver me north
during wild impatient
migration

I can't sleep
on account of daydreams

while in the principal's office

it's some kid's birthday

and his apparent

lack of concentration

will ruin his ability

to become a paramedic

when he grows up

VI.

To avoid doing homework
I dumped my books
in the mailbox

but the mailman
caught on
and began
delivering them
to my house

I almost went down
but Four Square saved me

during a recess

of satisfaction

free sky and

lightening

come cool

me down

in the artificial

glimmer

of paintbrush

strokes

I leave the

burning world

behind

PART FOUR: WHAT'S WRONG WITH YOU

1.

I tried to divide
my (imaginary) cake
into even pieces
but it came out wrong

it always comes out wrong

I am submerged by voices

bellowing billowing borrowing

confusion of B words dictated

at 1000 miles per hour

right through me

in me and out me

never lodging

where they are

supposed to

when I was trying

to find out

the least common

denominator

my heart blasted

so violently in my chest

I nearly fell over

backwards in my seat

told to pay attention

while *I actually was* paying attention

II.

"What's wrong with you?"

those 4 words
obliterate
any other thought:

drown out
ancient civilizations
drown out
the capital of Kansas
drown out
the colors of the rainbow
drown out
The Bill of Rights
drown out
semi colons

drown out

run-on sentences

drown out

capitalization

drown out

The War of 1812

drown out

Alexander Hamilton

drown out

The Emancipation Proclamation

drown out

Manifest Destiny

drown out

Ulysses Simpson Grant

drown out

my honor

those 4 words
become what I become

4 words
that define me

despite all of my
gorgeous attempts
to ignore them

despite my cousins

despite baseball

despite forts

despite climbing phone poles

despite swimming

despite beaches

despite boats

when I grow up
I want to be

any other words

but those

III.

Though every morning I cry
so deeply, so intently
hoping to jar my mother
into giving up

I can't wear her down

If only I could learn
The Theory of Evolution
I would have a better chance
at survival

but there is no one

to equip me

with such skills

as they are all out

fending

for themselves

I can't sleep on account of Charles Darwin

only in the temporary mercy

of gym equipment

am I able to forgive myself

I almost went down

but basketball saved me

A cloud over the rain
reimburses my family
for having provided me
with shelter

where otherwise
Strait A students
line up perfectly
in their award-ridden
uniforms

I can't sleep on account of spelling bees

song in my head
reminds me of summer
while the counselor
waits outside of science class
to ambush me

my heart sings
momentarily upon
the broken winds
cloudless skies
as I count down
the 83 days
until June 22

I am lying next to Michael

on the sand

in the relief

of sunshine

but when I open my

eyes I look down

to a menacing sheet

of blanks

with unanswered

questions

I frantically manage

to fill in

the letters sting

coming up

and I regret

having to vomit

beautiful words

upon command

see them destroyed

by ignorant authority figures

who have no business

standing in front

of my class

inside (random)

explanations

some kids

experience

ecstasy

while I am

only buried

deeper into

my inability

to solve

equations

When I grow up

I want to slither out

from this unbearable skin

and shed

all that I have been

forced to carry

unnecessarily

the weight

of division

and multiplication

I want to strain

my muscles like

the story of Atlas

who held up

the entire world

with his hands

instead I feel myself

collapse into a puddle

of melted wings

that have accidentally

flown too close

to the sun

I can't sleep on account of the Greek Gods

IV.

Since I failed

to turn in

my homework

for the 4th

straight day

I am not allowed

to go on the

field trip to

Sturbridge Village

with the

rest of the class

where pilgrims

will re-enact

The Last Supper—

take us through

their medicinal

herb gardens

in costumes

as characters

who bake pies

tend to chickens

in 1620

the worst part

is that the girl

with cancer

will be made fun of

on the bus

and nobody

will be there

to defend her

when they steal

her wig and play

keep away

while she tries

not to cry—

and I will miss

the chance

to punch

those bullies

in their fat faces

while simultaneously

showcasing

every

swear word

that

I know

my stomach threatens

to revolt

under such disturbing

circumstances

but since my name

begins with L

I will have to wait

hours

while the A-F's

line up outside

the nurse

who already

suspects

me

of

lying

V.

When I grow up
I want to be drafted
into an imaginary
army
who is hired
to protect
fling grenades
into enemy
territory

the promise
of heavy artillery
and retaliation
sustains me

yet the cruel

ambush

of faulty

neurotransmitters

gets me expelled

and the principal

is in no way

open

to suggestions

other than

the wild ride

of delivery

up my
bloodstream
soaked
in chemicals

I can't sleep on account of the medicine

Sentences
come whizzing
past me
like bullets
in a gangster
movie and
I feel like
I am being
shot at
by a spray
of misfired
words

since my initial
response is to
duck I scramble
under my desk
for cover—
which is
misinterpreted
as a hostile
act

and soon
I am escorted
down the hallway
to the present
incompetent
commander
in chief

how many

letters

of

apology

could I

possibly

write

in

one day?

meanwhile

it's my

brother's

birthday

and I am

stuck

in detention

while everyone

else

eats cake

PART FIVE: REINCARNATION

I.

While everyone else
learns to read
I bury spelling words
in the back yard
hoping they will grow
into something beautiful
that I can understand—
exotic teas and spices,
jasmine, cardamom,
pepper—

so that I can prevent
the European explorers,
Magellan
from sailing to the New
World in hopes of
finding

mercenaries

which live in

my boiling bloodstream

are impossible to control,

turn my face

red

gather up

spears for

my survival

When the Taino

reached out

in curiosity

to touch

the end of

Columbus' sword

their fingers

were sliced

in his amusement

slaughtered 4 million

on Haiti

wiped out

nearly completely

an entire

population

when I grow up I want to be re-incarnated

I want to return

as a slave

in my next life

and ride that

ship of disaster

with my hands

and feet chained

and shackled

back to

the old world

face down

the Spanish king

before he has the chance

to send explorers

to the New World

in search of

treasures

and if Christopher

Columbus

cuts off

my hands

for not

finding

enough

gold

I will use

my re-incarnation

to kill him

back

the next time

I bleed to death

vultures

will swoop

down upon

me and

carry me up

to heaven

(sky)

and like in

an ancient

myth

I will become

a constellation

that my children

in the future

will gaze up at

and wish

upon

II.

Suddenly
I want to hurry up
and die
so that I can
use my next life
to be brave,
heroic even

I want to
return to
this world
fixed,

capable

to feel
uplifted
by my own
intentions

rewarded
for my
efforts

in my next life
I want to be
swaddled
in baby blankets
by tender hands

sung to sleep
at naptime—

I want to
stand up
in my chair
and shout out
the right
answer

to be showered

in

gold

stars

all the way home

Lori Lubeski is the author of *Dissuasion crowds the slow worker; STAMINA; Obedient, A body; eyes dipped in longitude lines; Undermined,* and *pilgrimage foliage.* She collaborated with printmaker Jakub Kalousek on TRICKLE and *Sweet Land,* and on the forthcoming *estranged domain,* and with artist Jeannette Landrie on *Has the river of the body risen.* Recent work can be found in *Let The Bucket Down, Solstice*, and *Pangyrus.* Lori lives in Boston, where she teaches at Curry College.

Made in United States
North Haven, CT
05 December 2023